my very first
Christmas Carols

Written and compiled by Lois Rock
Illustrated by Alex Ayliffe

LION
CHILDREN'S

Let Us Travel to Christmas

Let us travel to Christmas

By the light of a star.

Let us go to the hillside

Right where the shepherds are.

Let us see shining angels

Singing from heaven above.

Let us see Mary cradling

God's holy child with love.

Contents

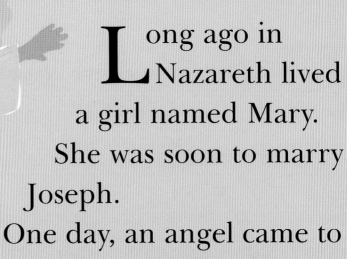

Long ago in
Nazareth lived
a girl named Mary.
She was soon to marry
Joseph.

One day, an angel came to
visit her.

'God has chosen you,' said the angel. 'You are
going to have a baby: God's own son – Jesus.'

Mary was astonished, but she
knew what to do.

'I will do what God wants,'
she said.

In a dream, the angel spoke to Joseph. 'Marry Mary,' said the angel. 'Take good care of her and her baby.'

'I will do what God wants,' Joseph agreed.

Months went by.

Then came more news: Mary and Joseph had to go to Bethlehem.

It was just at the time when her baby was about to be born.

O Little Town of Bethlehem

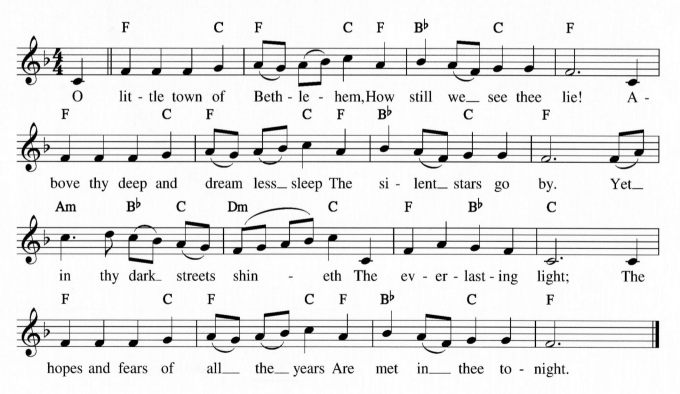

O lit - tle town of Beth - le - hem, How still we_ see thee lie! A -
bove thy deep and dream less_ sleep The si - lent_ stars go by. Yet_
in thy dark_ streets shin - eth The ev - er - last - ing light; The
hopes and fears of all_ the_ years Are met in_ thee to - night.

Mary Had a Baby

F   C⁷   F   C⁷

Ma-ry had a ba-by,   Yes,   Lord.   Ma-ry had a ba-by,   Yes, my Lord.

F   B♭   Am   F   G⁷ C⁷ F

Ma-ry had a ba-by,   Yes,   Lord. The   peo-ple keep a-com-ing Down in   Beth-le-hem.

What did she name him?

Yes, Lord.

What did she name him?

Yes, my Lord.

What did she name him?

Yes, Lord.

The people keep a-coming

Down in Bethlehem.

Mary named him Jesus,

Yes, Lord.

Mary named him Jesus,

Yes, my Lord.

Mary named him Jesus,

Yes, Lord.

The people keep a-coming

Down in Bethlehem.

Silent Night

Away in a Manger

The cattle are lowing, the baby awakes,

But little Lord Jesus, no crying he makes.

I love thee, Lord Jesus!

Look down from the sky,

And stay by my side until morning is nigh.

Be near me, Lord Jesus, I ask thee to stay

Close by me for ever, and love me, I pray.

Bless all the dear children in thy tender care,

And fit us for heaven to live with thee there.

On the hillside near Bethlehem were shepherds.

They were watching over their sheep all through the night.

It was dark.

Scary animals were howling and prowling.
Then something astonishing happened.

The First Nowell

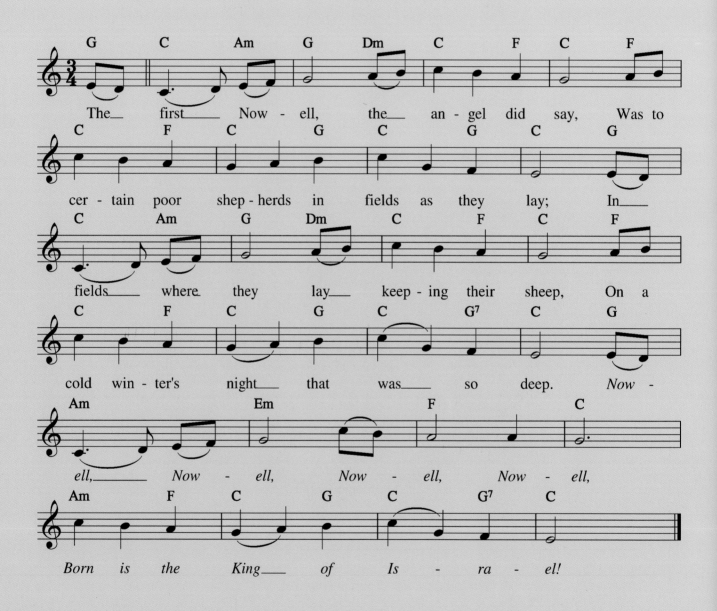

The— first— Now - ell, the— an - gel did say, Was to
cer - tain poor shep - herds in fields as they lay; In—
fields— where they lay— keep - ing their sheep, On a
cold win - ter's night— that was— so deep. *Now -*
ell,— Now - ell, Now - ell, Now - ell,
Born is the King— of Is - ra - el!

They looked up and saw a star,

Shining in the east, beyond them far;

And to the earth it gave great light,

And so it continued both day and night.

Nowell, Nowell, Nowell, Nowell,

Born is the King of Israel!

While Shepherds Watched Their Flocks

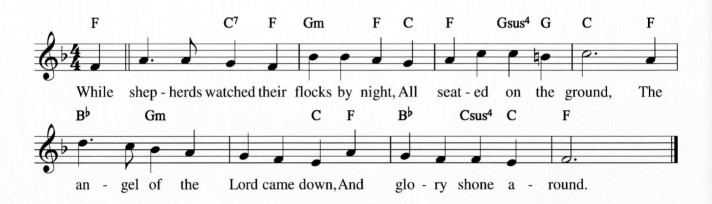

While shep-herds watched their flocks by night, All seat-ed on the ground, The
an - gel of the Lord came down, And glo - ry shone a - round.

'Fear not,' said he, for mighty dread

Had seized their troubled mind;

'Glad tidings of great joy I bring

To you and all mankind.'

19

From far away came travellers. They were following a bright star.

'It is a new star,' said the first.

'It is telling us a message,' said the second.

'It is a sign that a new king has been born,' said the third. 'We must go and bow down to him. We must take him gifts.'

They brought with them gold, frankincense and myrrh.

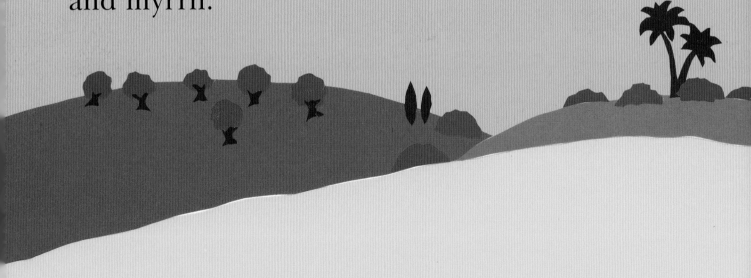

We Three Kings

O Come, All Ye Faithful

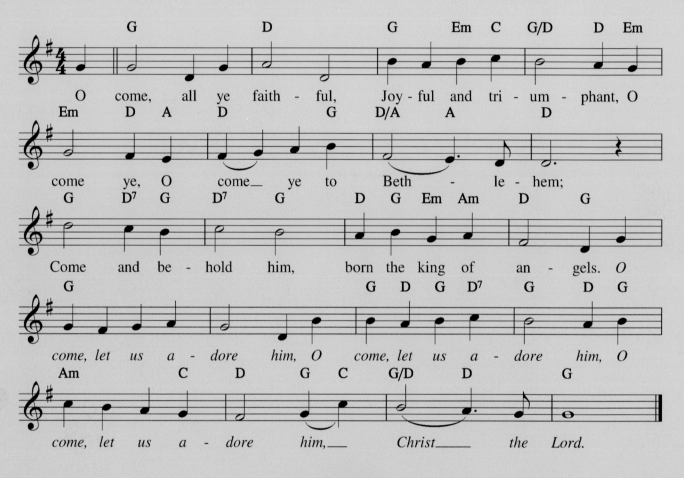

Go Tell It on the Mountain

Go tell it on the moun - tain, Ov - er the hills and ev - 'ry- where,

Go tell it on the moun - tain That Je - sus Christ is born. While

shep-herds kept their watch-ing ov - er wander-ing flocks by night, Be -

hold from out of hea - ven, There shone a ho - ly light._____

Go tell it on the mountain,

Over the hills and everywhere,

Go tell it on the mountain

That Jesus Christ is born.

And lo, when they had seen it,

They all bowed down and prayed,

Then travelled on together

To where the babe was laid.

Go tell it on the mountain,

Over the hills and everywhere,

Go tell it on the mountain

That Jesus Christ is born.

We Wish You a Merry Christmas

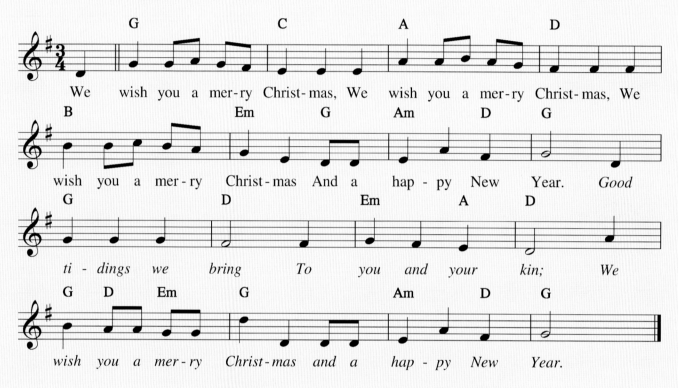

We wish you a mer-ry Christ-mas, We wish you a mer-ry Christ-mas, We wish you a mer-ry Christ-mas And a hap-py New Year. *Good ti - dings we bring To you and your kin; We* wish you a mer-ry Christ-mas and a hap-py New Year.

The Stars That Shine at Christmas

The stars that shine at Christmas

Shine on throughout the year;

Jesus, born so long ago,

Still gathers with us here.

We listen to his stories,

We learn to say his prayer,

We follow in his footsteps

And learn to love and share.

All Through the Night

Sleep, my child, and peace attend thee,

All through the night;

Guardian angels God will send thee,

All through the night.

Soft the drowsy hours are creeping,

Hill and vale in slumber sleeping,

I my loving vigil keeping,

All through the night.

Traditional Welsh prayer

Track listing:

1. *Let Us Travel to Christmas*

2. *Long ago in Nazareth…*

3. O Little Town of Bethlehem

4. Mary Had a Baby

5. Silent Night

6. Away in a Manger

7. *On the hillside near Bethlehem…*

8. The First Nowell

9. While Shepherds Watched Their Flocks

10. *From far away came travellers…*

11. We Three Kings

12. O Come, All Ye Faithful

13. Go Tell It on the Mountain

14. We Wish You a Merry Christmas

15. *The Stars That Shine at Christmas*

16. *All Through the Night*

The CD was produced by Andy Harsant for the ICC Media Group and features the voices of Alyx and Mia Gilham, Amanda and Anna Osbourne and Lydia Horne.

Acknowledgments
'Let Us Travel to Christmas' (page 2) and
'The Stars That Shine at Christmas' (page 30)
are by Lois Rock, copyright © Lion Hudson.

O Little Town of Bethlehem
Words: Bishop Phillips Brooks (1835–93)
Tune: Collected and adapted by Ralph Vaughan Williams
(1872–1958)

Mary Had a Baby
Words and tune: Traditional West Indian

Silent Night
Words: Joseph Mohr (1792–1848)
Translation from German: Anonymous
Tune: Franz Grüber (1787–1863)

Away in a Manger
Words: Anonymous
Tune: W.J. Kirkpatrick (1838–1921)

The First Nowell
Words and tune: Traditional English

While Shepherds Watched Their Flocks
Words: Nahum Tate (1652–1715)
Tune: Este's Psalter (1592)

We Three Kings
Words and tune: John Henry Hopkins (1820–91)

O Come, All Ye Faithful
Translation from Latin: F. Oakley (1802–80)
Tune: John Francis Wade (1711–86)

Go Tell It on the Mountain
Words and tune: Traditional English

We Wish You a Merry Christmas
Words and tune: Traditional English

Text by Lois Rock
Illustrations copyright © 1999, 2003, 2005 Alex Ayliffe
This edition copyright © 2007 Lion Hudson

The moral rights of the author and illustrator
have been asserted

A Lion Children's Book
an imprint of
Lion Hudson plc
Wilkinson House, Jordan Hill Road,
Oxford OX2 8DR, England
www.lionhudson.com
ISBN 978 0 7459 6034 0

First edition 2007
10 9 8 7 6 5 4 3 2 1

A catalogue record for this book is available
from the British Library

Typeset in 22/30 Baskerville BT
Printed and bound in China